TRANSVERSALES

TRANSVERSALES

MICHAEL GESSNER

BLAZEVOX[BOOKS]
Buffalo, New York

TRANSVERSALES
by Michael Gessner

Copyright © 2013

Published by BlazeVOX [books]

Printed in the United States of America

Interior design and typesetting by Geoffrey Gatza
Cover Art: Picasso, "Femme au feuillage"

First Edition
ISBN: 978-1-60964-147-4
Library of Congress Control Number: 2013942421

BlazeVOX [books]
131 Euclid Ave
Kenmore, NY 14217

Editor@blazevox.org

publisher of weird little books

BlazeVOX [books]

blazevox.org

21 20 19 18 17 16 15 14 13 12 01 02 03 04 05 06 07 08 09 10

BlazeVOX

Other Works by Michael Gessner

ARTIFICIAL LIFE

BEAST BOOK

THE CUSTODIAN'S JOURNAL

EARTHLY BODIES

GLASS

LETTERS

ON LOCATION, ESSAYS OF PLACE

SURFACES

THE WRITER'S CIRCLE

Grateful acknowledgment is made to those publications in which some of these poems first appeared:

Ann Arbor Review: "Moonstruck," "Poem"

The Blue Guitar: "Letter to a Poet," "Père Lachaise," "Rain," "The Return"

Cavalier Literary Couture: "The Keys of Paris," "Six Spanish Girls on the Streets of Cambridge"

The French Literary Review: "Place des Vosges," "Le Moulin de la Vierge"

Glimpse (Toronto): "Voltaire's Cap"

Nimrod International Journal of Prose and Poetry: "Thoth," "Seshat"

North American Review, "Sex Education"

Pacific Review: "Ferns: A Study"

Paterson Literary Review: "Winter Reading"

Rue des Beaux-Arts (Paris): "Wilde's Tomb"

The Yale Journal of Humanities in Medicine: "Washed Out"

"I Had Your Book" was chosen as a finalist by the judges of *Goodreads*.
"The Keys of Paris" and other poems were recorded in radio broadcast, KXCI – Tucson, February 20, 2012. Numerous poems from this collection were first read at Casa Libre en la Solana, Tucson, "Changing Hands" Tempe, University of Arizona, Tucson, and Cambridge University.

CONTENTS

ENCLAVES

The Steps of Montmartre, Unfinished Business
   & the Tenth Muse.. 15
Paper Moon... 16
Woman with Leaves.. 18
Rain.. 19
Place des Vosges... 20
The Markets of Seine-Saint-Denis..................................... 22
Ceinture Rouge... 25
Le Select.. 26
Communards.. 27
Le Moulin de la Vierge.. 28
Theatre.. 29
The Keys of Paris.. 30
The Abandoned Convent at Seine-Saint-Denis............... 31
Lemons.. 32
Père Lachaise... 33
Wilde's Tomb... 34
The Return.. 35
Salon d'Automne... 36
Petits Cailloux.. 37

RECURSIVE SELVES

Glossolalia... 41
Occupy: The Vatican... 42
Messengers of Art.. 44
Voltaire's Cap.. 45
Optimal Conditions.. 46
Film.. 47
Then... 48
Hard Art.. 49
Subject... 50
Glass Canes.. 51
Palmettos.. 52
Sunbonnet with Flowers.. 53
Boy in the Boat... 54
Poem.. 55
Letter to a Poet... 56
Moonstruck.. 57
I Had Your Book... 58

Six Spanish Girls on the Streets of Cambridge 59
Acts & Dispositions 60
French Tile 61
The Poem of Death 62
Those We Never Knew 63
Nothing Will Help 64
Friends 65
The Innocents at Sandy Hook 66
The Masters 67
Circulation 69
Returning Spell 70
Coal 71
Washed Out 72
Cigar Rings 73
Ferns: A Study 75
Eunuchs at Sunrise 77
Thoth 78
Seshat 80
Winter Reading 81
Walt Whitman's Novel 82
Looking for Picasso on eBay 83
La Belle Époque 84
Sex Education 85
Passion Bracelet 86
My Internet Family 87
Gold Stars 88
Geographics 89
Book of Sand 90
Roller Derby 91
Sleeves at the 13th Step 93
Magnificat 94
Staircase at Sceaux 95

TRANSVERSALES

ENCLAVES

THE STEPS OF MONTMARTRE, UNFINISHED
BUSINESS & THE TENTH MUSE

At the base of the stairs of Foyatier, the flâneur with the pink
cape shuffles a bit, & otherwise remains stationary taking in
the scene—it is unseasonably cool, a late morning, like no
other—while artifice is off pursuing the crowd, & promises
what it can only promise, a complete thing which is a packet
and as a packet it is all it is or could ever be, & promises no
other self. It is a political act. It is commerce, the exchange
of utilities consuming a measured period. And here, in late
morning when mist suffuses the steps of Montmartre,
the stroller is not a geometer of respectability, rather as in any
puritan state, a vagrant, the figure of indolence, the image
of the unfinished work & thus liberation & unformed selves,
an operative feature, a prospect from which the tenth muse
rebels & rebels from this prospect alone, alone as the flâneur
in this particular morning at the base of the steps of Foyatier
in his pink cape taking it all in. Here, the tenth muse is not
Sappho or Bradstreet, it is ambition. It is the commoner with
ready ax, who calls house to house, into the abodes of the
poem, dragging a cornucopia of hearts. Mnemosyne is grieving;
Père Lachaise is not coming along as planned, monuments
are in stages of ruin. Clio is to blame. But it is that other
one, the last born, the runaway, the collector, who cannot
abide what must remain incomplete & thus the perfections,
O Chimaera, the flourish of half and only half of the funerary
palm, the one snowflake dissolving on the heat of the adolescent's
arm, the discovery of escalators, the body within the body,
will within will, the spikes of light in a cold pond
where gold carp gather; what remains on the tongue
after wine or word, or frozen corpse.

PAPER MOON

Art gives form to the invisible.
—André Malraux

It has been my wish, rather it has been desire's wish, which I have called mine without understanding it, tho' it is desire nonetheless, as if I am desire speaking, & desire has led me to the desk of the concierge, Rudi, at Hôtel Saint Dominique to ask how to access the roof to get a better view of this section of 7ème. No, the elevator goes only to the fourth floor, & access to the roof is by stair and for the maintenance staff only, so you can't go there. Didn't I see workmen only this morning taking up materials? They are building something on the roof, yes? Hmmm. This is not generally known. We do not want to disturb our visitors. Maybe it is scaffolding, maybe it is for repair, or maybe it is a work of art, a diversion for the guests. Here, Rudi gives his perfunctory smile & returns to the paperwork on his desk.

Across the street in O'Brien's Irish Pub, I imagine the form of the new work—a diorama—*bricolage*—interior oscillating walls— with a surface like the surface of the paintings I had seen recently in art museums, the minute, geometrically symmetrical crackling of say, Tiepolo, a parchment, like the back of my hands, (only a recent development,) the texture of the materials through which we inhabit this world & which assume us into the world of cooperative conditions which is taking place now, as it has always, even if we only imagine its knowing, as we are known by it, source & field of dissolving renewal, always attracting us onward.

Sometime during the next Guinness Stout, which, if taken after fasting for several hours, has a smoky finish on the palate with a curiously suggestive edge of chocolate-charcoal, & some chatter with the bar host, there is my Corona, a Cubana Romeo y Julieta from the tabac shop which the woman retrieves from a glass case, & since I've become a regular customer, she pinches the foot to know if it is dry or spongy, smiles over her shoulder, & continues down the row to find one sufficiently resilient, which I now smoke half in & half out of the open shutters—I may sit on a chair positioned between O'Brien's floor & the sidewalk—still looking up with an occasional caress at the back of my head, a palm of air—as if I could see something on the roof, & seeing only the workman enter & leave the building with more materials—& since it is early evening & I have been up very early thinking about the scaffolding, making some notes for another project—all the projects are poems it turns out, or some connections among them as if they are reaching out to embrace each other—the word 'project' is used only for my dear friends who do not care to understand poems & would make an issue of my interest in them, an entertainment among themselves—& smoke the Corona down to its bitter leaves, which puts me in mind of the leaves of Daphne, when pursued by Apollo, transfigured into a laurel tree, *Laurus nobilis,* of all things, & thus those leaves in Picasso's "Femme au feuillage," & the history of memory in my hand, then return to the hotel room to lie on the bed where I am swept up in sleep still imagining what art is taking place on the roof. I ascend the stairs now & in the morning.

WOMAN WITH LEAVES

—Plaster, 1934. Private collection.

Objet de rebut. Let not even fools fool themselves,
the pregnant tension underlying the page; the pages
that flitter about the mind, thin leaves on display
like thin skin that breaks with age & blood cracks
& Amazons flow. These things slide along the page,
& open paper-thin wings, bat & butterfly, thin fingers
of the hand, caressing carp, the fish's fins, (the woman's
shoulder on the dark steps of the Metro in Seine-Saint-Denis
flipping mutant flesh-leaves for coins,) the outstretched fist,
the sign of protection & threat the runaway has assumed
in her leaves, invitation to the House of Image, the Biological
Theatre, leafy Eros, a welcoming that cannot be entirely
withdrawn, & thus the display of violence is saddened
& weakened, & the girl-tree imagines she has become
part of the canopy, the boxy head, a camera recording
everything, the mouth a cave, the tongue a bell, the heart
that beats-out words for the heart's tongue to tell, the mouth
full as if volume itself, the vowels alone, swollen leaves,
were mouth's meaning, & other leaves, those on the branch
over the breast shiver on apart, alone.

RAIN

It's been raining all day, raining in suburbs & in city parks
& continues in sheets across avenues, stalling traffic,
bouncing in waves off glacial curbs, & will, in turns,
reduce itself to a patter, then to finger-taps—tap—tap—
tap—drops down gutters and down spouts, only to gather
strength for the next downpour or the next—raiment after
raiment—breaking levees, flooding villages, sweeping them
out to sea, it is raining somewhere always, even now rains rain on
tin sheds & tile roofs, it rains in the barrio & in the banlieue,
& in the financial district, rains rain on the roof of Le Moulin
de la Vierge & the lovers who wait inside, on the glass domes
of arcades, & there is rain on the steps of Montmartre, & on the
abandoned convent in Seine-Saint-Denis, over the chartreuse
lichen and the ochre lichen on stone walls, but here this morning it
is raining over my house, a monologue of rain, & therefore it is
raining too where you are, & the rains are not the tears of infant
angels for our world's sake, they are not the rains of Zeus, or
another god inseminating the fields of Mother Earth, or clouds of
science, they are the patterings of an unknown companion, lost
and distant, now returned to wrap this house in sheets of itself.

PLACE DES VOSGES

for Michel Moisan

In the oldest square in Paris, in the Marais, a monument
is being built, a monument to all the monuments,
greater than any, a monument to the culture of invention,
invention transformed, a monument grander than the Panthéon,
that final cradle built by the masons of the Creuse.

It is a perpetual spiral turning ever upwards, revolving with murals
commemorating those who made Paris, the Paris of the senses,
who maintain it and keep it alive, without which there could not be
another Paris, there could not be the musée imaginaire, and here
in this square there is a spiral of revolving images and colors
unseen, for those who put ideas into the geometries of materials,
the creators of Lescot, Lemercier, Haussmann.

Without the labor of the unknown there would be no grand
palais—no grand e'toile—no grand boulevard—no grand
bibliothèque—no grand basilique—no grand école—no grand
arc—no grand jardin—no grand menagerie—no grand institut—
no grand académie—no grand cimetière—no grand tour (with its
72 gold names)—no grand musée—no grand cité de lumière

No, no Louvre, no Orangerie, no Orsay, no Musée des Beaux-Arts,
no Sacré-Cœur, no plaque with gold lettering for Apollinaire above
the brasserie, no stone for Eluard, no name on Hugo's door, or the
door of Gautier, no Bateau-Lavoir, no 27 rue de Fleurus, no
Sorbonne, no Odéon, no home for Dior, Guerlain, Vuitton, no
Sainte-Chapelle. And they, the builders, too poor to live where
they built, build always for others, homes for others, memorials
for others, statues for others. They build and repair and serve
and then return by night to districts outside the Paris they built
and where they cannot live.

Ceinture Rouge, noose of Paris.

To them, in this oldest square in Place des Vosges,
their monument will exceed all others and will overshadow
the statue of Louis XIII, and will draw its energies
from the vigor of the builders and from the spirit
of communes and from the descendants of the Communards,
defenders of Paris, and this turning narrative of murals in colors
yet unknown will be seen only by the pure, the poor, the laborers,
and will outlast the Panthéon and the venerable entombed therein.

THE MARKETS OF SEINE-SAINT-DENIS

The Metro shoots out of Paris—an eel through
a winding cave—gaining speed, the urgency to get
to where it must go. In the crowded car we grip
the balance pole. There is a gang of boys
who stare at us as if we were invaders, ghosts
of one tyranny or another, come back to haunt
(*honte*) with another plan for oppression.

November 23;27, 1870

> *For two days Paris has been living on salt meat.*
> *A rat costs 8 sous . . . . Pâtés of rat are being made.*

December 1, 1870

> [a friend] *came to see me today. We ate bear meat.*
> *. . . . stag, and bear, and antelope—presents from*
> *the Jardin des Plantes, [La Ménagerie].*

> — V. Hugo

We hurtle on toward the end of the line and deboard
at Seine-Saint-Denis. The boys are the first off, and wait
on the platform for the new arrivals. One will shout to a
woman stepping onto the train—she has lost something,
and must attend to it—while she turns, and the doors are
closing, another boy grabs her purse as the doors shut
and the Metro pulls away. They run up the stairwell laughing.
We pass a mutant mother on the stairs in the damp passageway,
under a light dull as an egg in a wire cage. She sits hunched
by the wall. There is a rusted can for coins by her feet,
and a baby cradled in her lap. She stares into the eyes
of the subway voyeurs, exposing her right shoulder;
crossing her breast with her left hand, she flips
her fingers at the three fleshy fins from some aberration,
thalidomide, or a remnant of the aquatic life.

December 24, 1870

It is freezing. Ice floes are floating down the Seine.

December 31, 1870

Yesterday I ate rat. We no longer have horse to eat . . . . I am beginning to suffer pains in the stomach. We are eating the unknown.

January 3, 1871

Moon. Intense cold. The Prussians bombarded St. Denis all night.

Here we've come to the home of the homeless, Séquano
Dionysiens, the grounds of the kings and queens exhumed
by revolutionaries, come to the labyrinth of tented markets
that sell living creatures for consumption, what creeps or runs
or crawls; crickets, monkeys, turtles, horse organs, pig intestines,
insects—siege food—meats of unidentifiable origins, carp
and eel and octopus among jars of chamomile flowers,
vanilla beans, hibiscus leaves for *bissap* tea; absinthe
leaves for licorice tea. This is motif.

January 12, 1871

We had elephant steak for luncheon today.

We cannot stay long, never after dark, the guide shows us
the Basilica of St. Denis and hurries us along to the markets.
They are festivals of brightly colored tents with every exotic thing
the heart desires. We must hold our belongings tightly to our
chests, leave no thing loose or it will be ripped away, never
look eye-to-eye for you may become prey, put your cameras away,
hide the slings, hold your handbag to your body. Do not reveal
your hands or let them hang by your sides.

We walk about the edge of the rings within rings of booths
packed together, we could go deeper but it was not advised.

It was not advised by the concierge at our hotel in Paris,
not advised to come here in the first place, and we went anyway,
and we did not know why. During our walk from the Basilica
to the markets, there was an interview. What did the foreigners
make of this region of the Red Belt, how startling and varied,
how multi-cultural, how novel. It was as if we did not know
poverty; that we were charmed by cheap rugs and scarves,
underwear, motor oil and mouse traps. This was televised
on France 24; later, a German affiliate ran the interview
with background footage of the fires set during the last riot,
as if poverty is uncommon, when it is everywhere.

Some streets are named after Communards, and others who
served the Paris Commune; Jean Baptiste Clément, Gustave
Courbet, Louise Michel, Jules Vallès.

CEINTURE ROUGE

Splotches of red
flash by
mill & countryside,
red blades,
someone's door,
a trailer,
& in cities,
red scarves,
winter faces,
red with cold,
red with rouge,
red with rage,
& red window frames
of mace manufacturers,
red eyes, red as rain,
red as trout roe,
the tips of tracer rounds,
red as blood
drained from pale
forms that wander
though markets
among bodies
of animals
hung from hooks.

LE SELECT

Almost every afternoon from spring to fall she may be
seen at the same table ordering the espresso first, then
a Malbec, or two if it is a good day, or if it is a bit
brisk, or if it drizzling over the canopy, otherwise it's
the whites, especially during the summer months.
The order is followed by a silver cigarette & she allows
the smoke to drift upward casually from open lips,
otherwise she appears distant & indifferent. In this way,
sipping from cup & glass, two hours pass. Her gloves
are black gauze & she is here owing to a moderate
inheritance; for many years the absentee proprietor
of L'École de Charme for privileged girls of subdued
energies, now mothers with summer homes on the coast.
Just down the street at another café is a man her age.
He wears a white jacket. They share the same condominium
building & do not know this since the building is imposing
& they are in different wings. Although here they share
the terrace of pavement. He is a retired officer of foreign
affairs. They will never meet; they would only see emptiness
in each other, when they would rather see the sleek, the curious,
the slight splendors, emaciated models, petty scams, & other
nuances of the street.

In the spring of 1871, and for about two months
following the Franco-Prussian War, the National
French Guard made possible the establishment of
"The Paris Commune." When their countrymen
came to collect cannons and machine guns, the
Guard barricaded the city. During "Bloody Week"
it is estimated that 20,000 to 50,000 French Guard
were executed; others later imprisoned or deported
to forced labor colonies. The Commune became
a rallying cry for the working class.

COMMUNARDS

Here they are again, the faithful dead.
They could be anyone, Spartans or Serbs,
Fenians, Nigerians, the "Freedom Fighters"
of any land, but these are different.
They have been uploaded for the world to see,
torn chests, disfigured faces, black and white
daguerreotypes, nude bodies on display,
electronic images in digital perpetuity.

They have been disgraced forever this way,
all bearded and boxed, subjects of one last
macabre prank or hoax before the grave.
They lay uncircumcised in their cheap board
caskets in rows set at an angle for the camera's
best exposure, some with black wreathes
pressed into dead fingers, held over hips,
placed around genitals as if in mockery.

Most are young as war dead are, and once bold,
without compromise, and their loves were set
aside, having taken up a cause that was
unattainable and basic as bread, slain by countrymen
as much as irony, and in these photographs
remain an epitaph to the strange prospects of victory,
more obscene than any corpse could be, ideals torn
easily as a body, a body torn easily as a spring plant.

LE MOULIN DE LA VIERGE

In the mill of the virgin, the local patisserie,
lovers wait in line with their loves,
they wait for *mille-feuille* , the buttery & brittle
thousand sheets with layers of light cream whipped
silly with the scent of raspberry,
for pastry cones and pastry shells,
of spun fluff in glass cases so they cannot float
away, & chiffon slippers lined with lemon froth,
bowls of macaroon puffs airy as cupid's cheeks,
& when the lovers are in love they are in love
with Paris, Paris glazed, & Paris powdered,
Paris of flaky cream horns,
Paris of vertiginous confection,
Paris Paris pastry crust.

THEATRE

Tonight it is theatre & it is theatre only. It is the culture
of spectacle. It is what is on the marquee. It is the theatre
of bell ringers, of grand boulevards, the chairs of brasseries
turned toward the street, toward the promenades of pedestrians,
the flowing scarves, the diatribe, the sweat of speakers on the
concrete stage of persuasion. It is the night of the illusionist,
the one black leaf stuck to the pavement with rain.

The mural of history is theatre, the gold statues in city squares
are theatre; the churches, theatre, the military in their engagements
& in their parades, the dramas that take us in, surround us, &
promise liberation, and so it is always, theatre marvelous, theatre
compelling, theatre corrupt, the monk in his cell in love with pity
& martyrdom is the theatre of the one soul, tremulous leaf, the
floating self, artist & diplomat, the industrialist & the national
community, all theatre, but for the act of labor alone without
consequence, for the anonymous, not as lawyers live in the theatre
of fabricated character & political trial, rather as one might find
in the eruptions of mountains, as if in rivalry with panoplies of
cosmic light, cataclysms, flamboyant effusions & death star
collisions, & tonight, here now, always, there is the theatre
of the poet & the poem.

THE KEYS OF PARIS

The lovers write their names on locks
then fasten them to the black chain-link fence
on both sides of the *Pont des Arts*,
that wooden footbridge over the Seine.

There are rows & rows of lovers' locks,
the chromium latches glint in the sun,
& the lovers, in a grand gesture of fidelity,
toss their keys into the river, & depart.

The keys lay on the bottom, sometimes turning
in wreathes of current, or they may remain
still for years, or they may roll,
crossing over one another.

THE ABANDONED CONVENT AT SEINE-SAINT-DENIS

Doors.

The guide must pound and pound on them until the edge
of his palm is flushed with pounding and the guard leaves
his station to unlock the wooden doors, centuries old, tall
and gothic and black and set in fluted channels in an arch
far above us. The doors, reluctant, creak and the guard
seeing his counterpart, the guide, motions us in. The doors
are closed and will remain closed until we have seen the nun.

Courtyard, the lichens.

Lichens, the lichens, chartreuse lichens and yellow lichens.
Rings circling over rings. Deckles of rust lichen and rose lichen
on the courtyard walls, deep golden lichen in miniature sunbursts,
walls crusted with splotches of lichen, *croute de pierre*. They are
everywhere; over the fieldstone courtyard, about the metal spouts
up which cats shinny to stalk the window sills for the sparrow too
sick to fly. The window has a blue frame, there the keeper tells us,
the old woman looked out every day at the workers who passed
her way, who occupied the apartments once inhabited by the
sisters of St. Botanica. The lichens create their own designs, seek
their own symbiotica, joining filaments, elective affinities extending
themselves into other identities by texture, the unknown chemical
callings of algae, even the purple plaque, isolated on the dry stone
fountain. When the workers returned, the last nun would still be
staring from her window, staring at the courtyard, the opposite
walls, the lichens, staring at space itself. One morning they filed by
and she was no longer there. The keeper maintains the empty
apartment now, cleaning the glass daily.

When it becomes dark the lichens sink into the darkness.
The few black pocks, the teals, dark to darker blue-green,
the grays, are the first to go, the rest surrender, glyphs
in ink into nightfall, nightfall and the moon, and as the moon
moves its light ricochets in phosphorescent tracers,
glimpses of silver bloom on walls, the courtyard,
the metal spouts, the locked doors.

LEMONS

On the way to Père Lachaise,
a fruit vendor told me the lemons
are edible & may be eaten whole,
but they must be accompanied
with sugar, preferably from dark grapes.

PÈRE LACHAISE

Leaves clatter down cobblestone streets like tin cups,
& empty souls move about the Sunday children
who laugh & chase each other down the streets
chattering after themselves, they give half-life
to this city of images, human & divine,
where no one lives & no one dies,
where families collect their young
at the end of their visit, & leave this place
to the leaves that swirl in wheels . . .

When Mars, the Gorgons, Lamia
& the warheads are sleeping,
& I am vacant, no longer thinking,
when all things are absent,
you arrive, a ghost anthology written in the dark,
of other lives, lovers, & lovers' art.

WILDE'S TOMB

But these, thy lovers, are not dead,
.... they will rise up & hear your voice,
and run to kiss your mouth.

—"The Sphinx"

In the garden of Père Lachaise,
city of the dead, we passed angels
covering their faces in shame,
& nineteenth-century trees, with tops bowed
as if their only purpose was to grieve,
& crossed the Transversales to Wilde's grave.

When lovers leave, they leave their kisses
glistening on the slab,
on impressions of lips themselves,
a tissue of strangers' cells
the conservators cannot leave alone,
& scrub the graffiti, as the plaque decrees
by law, no one can deface this tomb,
& still the images of lips remain,
dark gray stains of animal fat
imprisoned in limestone.

Lips are pressed as high as lovers
climb, against the Sphinx's ridiculous
headdress, on the carved trumpet
of fame, & on the cheeks of its voracious face
of mindless passion flying with eyes pinched tight,
that some farsighted lover tried to open
with lines from a red pen, like a blepharoplasty,
while others kissed its sybaritic mouth
to make a poem a prophecy.

So here is love alive
surviving the wreckage it survives,
a lipstick envelope of hearts on their flight
to some other place, less aware,
more receiving, a final Champ de Grâce.

THE RETURN

With a tour group closing in, we left Wilde's sphinx
where sentiment always is, & followed the Avenue Circulaire
to the wall of the Communards, then to a bench across from a
cenotaph, broke a baguette, & stared as mourners stare.

Behind the bench, a grassy hill, & behind it, a boulevard
we could not see, but from above, over the tiers of trees,
a French girls' choir gave its rehearsal from some high-rise;
angled notes folding & unfolding purely on decisions of air,

& went on like this for an hour or more, the repertoire
complete, the girls with ribbons in their hair, as if performing
for Experience for its own sake, bounced down stairs
to waiting cars, cafés & girly affairs.

Evening came. What was left but the long walk back,
a decanter of wine, house red, in one of those cafés on rue Cler.

SALON D'AUTOMNE

While napping, I noticed a crevasse
under my bed which led downward
to a roomy hollow covered in layers
of October, amber leaves in circulars,
enough to fill the mouths of the dumb
with paper tongues, & in the gallery,
between the pit & me,
masters of the immutable,
assembled with arms upheld
like trophy-tusks, each with an oversized
brush clenched in his teeth.

Every day they gather at the same hour,
like mastodons, to wait for a sound
to arise from the hollow below,
from that bed of paper tongues
all colored rose & gold & rose,
& perhaps with time, the leaves will dry
& curl into slight souls, rise upward
with some breath, a drift of breeze,
paper boats afloat.

PETITS CAILLOUX

The planter above Stein's grave holds small stones.
We looked about until we found two agates on the ground,
one black, the other amber, and set them in place
with our left hand like ancient Jews, to mark the place,
to say someone came here and someone thought of those below,
for Gertrude at her best, for Alice tucked in back without a view
like misplaced punctuation, and we prayed our prayers
for what lives souls take, for bad winters, dusty apartments,
war, shabby dress.

RECURSIVE SELVES

GLOSSOLALIA

In the columbarium of dead tongues,
each in a glass box with a bronze plate
stamped with the indecipherable
name of its owner, I can only imagine
how they howled over the ruins of past ages,
with the certain knowledge
their words would be kept
in the ancient libraries of Sumer or Ugarit,
in languages now lost or forgotten.

Even tonight, somewhere there is
a gospel tent, or a caravan stopped
for a meteor shower, to form a circle
on a mountain slope babbling
scrambled syllables, as if the dead
languages had returned, eloped
& married in multiples,
polygamous echoes on a journey
trying to make themselves known.

Aaron, a sandal maker, the younger brother
of Thomas, left his home urged by his parents
to search for his brother so as to return him
to his family, and on his journey witnessed
the Master cleansing the temple of lenders
and thus became a zealot of the cause and
was anointed as the thirteenth disciple, given
the power of proclaiming conscience through
the voice of the Master down the ages.

OCCUPY: THE VATICAN

Go, sell what you possess, and give to the poor
and you will have treasure in heaven . . .
—Matthew 19:21

Occupy the halls of government, empty of conscience, occupy
all properties dispossessed of compassion, occupy Wall Street,
surely, the Gold Coasts—Chicago and Hong Kong, Monte Carlo
and Côte d'Azur—occupy Madrid, Place des Vosges and the
Bourse, if you must, occupy the parks of the people in 108
countries, and the grand gardens of Powerscourt, Versailles, the
Boboli, but above all, occupy the Vatican.

Occupy that temple to the body of Christ to regenerate a soul that
has been abandoned, inhabit the basilica and the chapel void
of the beatitudes, where the dispossessed will find shelter.

In the square of St. Peter, melt the gold rings of cardinals,
auction all archives and art to feed the hungry, distribute crosiers
to the crippled so they may walk upright, clothe the naked
with vestments purchased with pennies from the poor,
created in Christ's name, tho' the creation of suffering is sin,
turn the pikes of the Swiss Guard into ploughshares,
and these things will lessen the afflicted and offer the gesture
of atonement on earth, *imago mundi*, while maintaining any article—
the stations, *The Pietà*—such as deemed necessary to their devotion.

Carve the sins of priests & bishops into the obelisk of Heliopolis,
may they lay prostrate before it, in the square, to pray
for forgiveness of the unforgivable, for their obscenities, for the
molestation of children, for requiring the faithful to overpopulate
themselves into a poverty that cannot know dignity, to pray to
Mary Blessèd Mother for the evictions of nuns made homeless
in their final years so as to settle legal disputes among the victims
of abuse, while hoarding treasures beyond measure, refusing
to release any object from any library, gallery or museum.

For those who occupy for justice's sake, theirs is the Kingdom
of Heaven.

MESSENGERS OF ART

More revolutionaries arrive tomorrow. Their
shadows may be seen on the horizon at night
fall. They promise to fulfill the claims that great
titles create, & do not give even when re-read.

All your familiars are strangers to me, just as
my familiars are strangers to you. So the human
wheels revolve like the shuffled pages
of telephone directories, spun in space, faceless

names, galaxies of titles from impressions,
the impressions made by what stands & moves
behind prototypes, the enduring assembly of new
revolutionaries, that appear one by one, then crisscross.

VOLTAIRE'S CAP

A student with time to kill
between classes, I dallied underground
in the Detroit Institute of Art
where I found Voltaire's cap
in a glass case in a corner
with other embroidered objects
of the period. It was white cotton lace,
like a skull cap. It would fit a baby's head.

I too, have hats, a rack of them,
straw for summer walking, the black band
stained with streaks of salt, a worn Panama
of my father's, some tennis caps,
& a dark blue felt for winter wear.

We could walk the museum in our hats,
walk the long halls, discussing perfection
over & over, then take the escalator of hats
to the garden floor café known for its pastry
& discuss the rich imaginary girls that show up

between classes, & your cap, the size of my fist,
empty of longing, & how the history of all things
is a collection of made of these.

OPTIMAL CONDITIONS

The landscapes of moons are silent
& do not move in the mind.

If people are talking about it then it matters.
If they are not talking, the subject is gone
& everyone becomes another time.

The trend seems to be, keep moving.
Join in the jumble parade, jumble up rods
of rebar, blocks of slump block, neon images,
those crates that keep re-surfacing, jackets,

the juggernaut, the discombobulated,
the cock-eyed, tumble until there is
in a collage a dimension, & the subjects
of popular political ideology have been

avoided once again for a prosperous angle
of sense before everyone stops talking, shuffle
fragments, but keep moving. Anything can be
precious.

FILM

The thin, multi-chromatic skin of bubbles is film's cast, the oil
slick on the water's surface from the powerboat ride you took
one evening with a friend I can't remember, on webs that span
docks & doors, the sheen on costumes of improvisation,
abandoned corpses, on tree & trunk, flossy reflections from moods
of weather & light, the film that joins film when surfaces caress
or collide, the film we see, the one of ourselves, slick celluloid,
the iridescence of the oily film on our skin, how it beckons
& floats with untraceable turnings, coppery nuances in the gold
haze about the summer stream at evening, the film of memory
memory makes, glossy photographs in plastic albums, the gleam
of new book jackets, shiny pages of birds & beaches, surfaces
of objects, sea shells, shimmer of lip gloss, the silk shirt I wore
last night, luster over morning moss, the surface of the moon.

THEN

Eurytion arrived at the outskirts of town near the landfill
of language which he regarded as an endless source of energy,
discharging diction at transonic speed so it was only the streak
seen in the sky, a vapor flash, & then piles of words assuming
forms otherwise discarded were it not for the attraction of their
gathering into cosmic shapes, appearances waiting for that old
flame, Personify, as Eurytion himself had been reformed from
Eurytus, fixed, & thus pursued the dead virgin bride through
the eternal until he had come to this, her resting place.
It was what transfixed him and brought him here
as it had brought me, observer of the paper exchange,
the financial times, the reappropriations, leaves of pulp
recolored, collections of mobiles trading like glossy playing
cards without faces in the dump.

HARD ART

They were never wrong, the hard of heart,
schools of gravel & flint
where hardness is the rule of art.

Among illuminated ruins
float fragments of the self,
mumblings of a sort who write
like Marquis de Sade, in his blood,
straight from the throat,
irresistible lines on winter streets,
cityscapes, clanging brass,
while others, dispossessed, remain
political prisoners huddling *en masse*
in dark corners, waiting for skylight.

SUBJECT

Without effusion the poet has no subject,
& is invisible as the ground must be
invisible, like a presence felt,
the sense of form, flashing its way.

GLASS CANES

The glass canes are hung
from a steel rod
in The Shop of The Sun.

One is blue,
another amber,

the strongest, clear glass.

PALMETTOS

In Bad Königshofen, in upper Bavaria
near a little village where my grandfather
was born—a man I never knew—there
is a church with dwarf palms outside.
I ask my friend, Mathias, why would there
be tropical plants this far north & he tells me
they were brought back by Crusaders
from the Holy Land, & these plants are their
descendants. Besides, he shrugs, they are
in planters & taken inside in winter. We
have villagers too, you know, whose ancestors
were in the Crusades, so this is not unusual.
'In history, things go this way, *nicht wahr*?

In Philadelphia at the Spring Garden House where
Poe lived, the curators—National Park Service
rangers—are fond of informing visitors that
the cats they see lurking outside the house
are the descendants of Virginia's Catterina,
& to pet them is like petting Catterina. In the
early winter of Virginia's death, in the cottage
at Fordham, the cat never left her bed, keeping
her warm along with her husband's military
cloak, and later, within days of Poe's own death,
Catterina, who habitually fasted in his absence,
gave up the ghost.

When I see the church cats—the kitchen help
feeds them—creep about the palmettos & mention
Catterina to my friend, Mathias, he tells me, 'So
this is how history remembers itself, *nicht wahr*?

SUNBONNET WITH FLOWERS

for V.H.

Set on a glass table like a summer
memorial, day's work done, a straw hat
with a blue ribbon meant for gardeners,
placed over stalks of irises,
the petals extend beyond the brim.

It could have been the perfect composition,
but some of the round top was worn through,
as though from sun, or harsh weather,
maybe chewed away by the family dog
when forgotten overnight in the back yard,

a chip from a gardener's fingernail
held to the light, something that was not missed.
Our absence should be as much,
the equivalence of image
the other side of memory.

BOY IN THE BOAT

The boy in the boat did not care
if he said the right word or if a word
was said, if he moved or if he did not,

indifferent & reclining on the bow,
as if enigma never seized him,
his eyes still covered with morning glaze,

adrift in the Pacific inlet, on still water
into the evening & each evening
was the same.

He wore my father's oversized shirt,
& like my son, we sometimes shared
that long & distant look of distraction,

there was this & something more,
I would always envy,
love & never understand,

in the boat he did not care
if he worshipped me
or some other minor god of the air.

POEM

One thing alone does not exist—oblivion.
                                    —Borges

The poet in a lawn chair by the side of the sea
had been reading another poet, perhaps Neruda,
and since it was summer and languid, and he had been
reading a long time, he fell to sleep.

When he woke, he called out to his wife to tell her
his dream, and when she did not answer, and no
one was about, and the house was empty and there was
only the sea, he took his pen and wrote:

The poem is always its own. It is true and it cannot die.
At our own death, from the chest, the treasury
of the poem, a baby dove, invisible,
flies out to find its flock in eternity.

LETTER TO A POET

Permit this brief intrusion
into a life of uncommon callings,
simply to say what I read this morning
shimmers like the gold foil musings
in the compositions of the Masters
of Sunlight, its memory reflects
in my palm, flake of tremulous gold.

MOONSTRUCK

At 2 a.m. Irish paces the hall.
I hear her collar tags when she shakes
and she shakes every few minutes
due to the fullness of the moon
my wife claims, and there is no place
where the dog is at rest,
not in her bed at the foot of our bed,
not on the couch downstairs
or in my son's abandoned room.

Maybe it is the moon pulling us
away from ourselves, an agitation
of the central nervous system. We too
are awake tonight and though we do not
pace the hall, we are restless
like the dog who cannot sleep,
and imagine a state of consolation,
a return to dreams: the silhouette
of Irish against a gray dawn dancing relevé.

I HAD YOUR BOOK

I had your book in my hand.
It told me everything about you,
the thin pages of the heart, the harried life,
and why you left yourself
for the time it took to create another.

Your book and I are the same,
like the peach blossom god
who wants to be created over and over,
who is silent and cannot say enough.

Just as memory surrounds devastation
making a loveliness of disaster
that floats over time like blossoms
over homes hurricanes collapsed,
or kaleidoscope dew over headstones,

When print vanishes, the stitching separates,
when the title fades and is no longer readable,
the knowledge of your book is in my hand,
the impression of the spine in the palm remains.

SIX SPANISH GIRLS

ON THE STREETS

OF CAMBRIDGE

Here for their summer programs,
to speak household French, or English,
they come arm in arm
chatting down King's Parade,
in the evening, after dinner,
& laugh together over the bridge of Cam,
then turn down a narrow street,

& I follow, leaving my own turning
far behind, in the plume of exuberance,
as if I were absorbed in their company,
before they break up, enter Clare College,
& go to their rooms
leaving the street & all that's in it
resounding with girlishness.

ACTS & DISPOSITIONS

These were long days, days of drought,
the wind snapping at nothing,
the dry death-rattle of the cicada,
& the dust-cones spinning

'round what growing things there were,
tearing at them, rearranging the composition
of the landscape, as though the air
was discontent with its season.

What was gathered here was gathered
on the dry land which could not prosper,
not even by expansion, without the acacia
& the poppy, juniper & mesquite.

Not for ourselves, not for our arrival
had we sought the high country
where the air quickens our breathing
with another story: electricity & the orchid,

apprenticed like a fossil-print to the promise
of a discovery greater than the last the voice
is prompted to give an explanation,
what the rain attempts to do

falling on the slate roof.
If the weather is heavy, the weather dense,
if the rain is long
in falling, 'round the carved serpents' heads,

there with the rain, something of the storm's
electric should linger,
compliant as statuary
about the story.

FRENCH TILE

The tenants next door are re-flooring their apartment
with porcelain. It is midnight-blue with sprays of silver
dust scattered here & there, as if looking down
on constellations.

In the evening when the tenants, a childless couple,
hold hands, objects among objects, they must imagine
themselves floating among endless stars.

THE POEM OF DEATH

This is the poem of death.
There is only one
and no other.

Every one is an occasion,
one way or another,
and the last poem is this poem of death.

It is an occasion like no other.
I will no longer lope after elegance,
beauty's body, or love's wonder.

I will be sorry for everything
I was, and for everything I was not.
I speak to you as if you were my brother.

I will forgive everyone.
Death will make this possible,
there will be no other.

Death was in the mind
before thought or love,
in ourselves and in our lovers.

The poem of death is speechless,
a companion will appear again
like another self, like your brother.

Enough now, enough has been said,
the spinning leaf will spin
like no other.

THOSE WE NEVER KNEW

What you said you said,
& will be rethought over time,
& what you know you know,
will be redefined by those
better read, more refined.

One day they too will arrive
& meet themselves on a corner
in a neighborhood they never knew,
& will talk your talk
until they talk just like you.

NOTHING WILL HELP

Nothing will help us now,
not country paths, not cement,
not the way of martyrs,
not the promise of gold lamps.

Nothing will help now,
not conversations with saints,
or old companions who have gone
down the thousand streets of the heart.

Nothing will help,
or stop the coming apart, the dry blue leaves
scattered down an empty street,
the thousand leaves of the heart.

FRIENDS

The friends I thought were friends were not,
they turned me in and left me out,
they used me up and then forgot.

And if there were others, witty, worthy, wise,
I did not know them, did not hear them call
my name, did not hear them sympathize

with my wishes or my dreams, or what was true,
they were not friends, they were not you.

THE INNOCENTS AT SANDY HOOK

Nothing can reach you now, not lead or steel,
or what life itself eventually reveals.

No more studies of kindness or courtesy,
not grace or charity, all is needless now.

All is needless now, sky, world, family
grieving for their bundles of purity,

now beyond disgrace, failure, winter streets,
of whatever attacks, and then retreats.

Classrooms emptied of children's things,
paper and paste, and love's imaginings,

bundles of peace, Christmas-blessed
with the unborn and the dead at rest,

nothing can reach you now, not lead or steel
or what life itself eventually reveals.

THE MASTERS

Fitzwilliam Museum, Cambridge

After rows of cuneiforms pressed
in salmon-colored clay, after exhibits
of gold-foiled glass on glass shelves,
aisles of marble heads, abducted thinkers,
and foreign patriots, cases
of painted fans and samplers
ancient girls made, after the displays of swords
and hammered armor pilfered from lands
philologists could not name,

we saw a group of children pass
under the Caryatids, then gather
in Gallery Three. All in red vests
and white collars, some stood, attentively,
others sat cross-legged on the carpet
faded with floral designs, a few on settees,
listening to their teacher explain how
the creators had affection for their art,
otherwise how could their art be?

The sunlight through the clerestory above,
suffused the plaster frieze, a cast
of the Elgin marbles, and onto scrolled frames,
poppyhead finials, and entered
the pores of statuary, the faces
of ancients, the flying creatures
of myth they made, and the red-vested
children, respectful, clean, as if the sun
was slowly purifying everything.

The teacher went on to explain
how artists live in a different world
when they work, a sacred place
and how the lives of the children too
could be the same, whatever their direction,

whatever they made, how the things
that surrounded them that day
were forms of affection, and the masters
themselves, objects of imagination.

CIRCULATION

I am certain of nothing but the holiness
of the Heart's affections . . .
                                    —Keats

The rounded heart's rhythm keeps momentum
with the cosmos, they are the same.

The wounded heart does not understand
circularity. It does not know sameness

even though they are one. It does not understand
the affection of death.

RETURNING SPELL

Blue light on blue leaves
on the trees & on the street
that is young & has nowhere
to go, so absorbed by its own
color it cannot care.

COAL

Just past the railroad tracks
the Oneida coal yard glistened
on my boy's route to school.
The fence was low, easy to jump
and then to roam among pyramids
of black rock, coal dust on the ground
like silver moon dust on the moon,
all to find the company's signature
on foil discs the size of quarters
thrown into the chutes as the coal
shot out, a fine souvenir, a trade item
with the Oneida chief himself
embossed in silver with his headdress
against a cobalt-blue background.

I showed up at school for morning mass
dirty as sin,
coal dust in god's house,
and worse, at home,
a course scoldings could not change,
and now I cannot look
at the silhouettes of mountains
against a pale night sky,
or see city light or moon light
without the smell of coal,
coal on my clothes, coal in my hair,
and on those foil wafers, hard won,
the grit remains
settled on all things.

WASHED OUT

My father stands in boxers,
back to the sea. He holds
my hand. I am five. We are a pair
on this Florida beach. We've remained
for years this way in black and white.

At forty-seven he looks 'washed out,'
a phrase I learned from him,
used by a generation without pigment
spray, or tanning booths, to explain
the pallor of the face in age,
its waxiness from lack of circulation,
its corollaries in cotton fabrics hung
too long in the sun,
or what hurricanes do to ports,
and the conch on the beach
bleached of color.

He was no longer 'in the pink,'
as his childhood chums would say
of each other when flushed
with health and expectation,
but not washed up, either,
not like the bloated things
that bellied-up and were pushed
away by tides, the undesirable
forms on the sand we stepped around.

Still we are here,
squinting against the sun,
still casting shadows.
In a few years I learned another phrase,
'Life is cheap,' he'd say,
odd, for one who held it so near.

CIGAR RINGS

Even now they are evidence of paradise,
paper bands kept in a favorite drawer,
fathers once gave their children to be worn
as rings, a convenient source of early
mythology, the Dutch Masters in their best
black puritan hats gathered around
a table discussing art, no doubt,
the Da Vinci brand for creative men,
Pleides, with a smoke destined
for the stars, & the royal bands
of American Indians holding clumps
of tawny leaf on either side
of an earthly globe over which Indian
Tabac ruled, & other myths too, Excalibur,
Romeo y Julieta, Montecristo, White Owl,
& promising a smoke affectionate as tough love,
Sancho Panza Extra Fuerte.

These exist in a pure state,
free of toxins, cancer, grief,
calmed, hand-rolled, leaf by leaf
chaste as the flower-women framed
in circles of gold foil, Flor de This
& Flor de That, Flor de Fantasie,
Flor de Forever, Athena of the Cameroon
wrapper & spicy ligero filler,
a smoke for the wise, & on the walls
of cigar bars, floating with his silken harem,
the sultan of smoke moves in clouds
from the best puros, judiciously holds
his Cubano Pilato, & the whole ensemble,
vessel & feathered fans, everything
carries the odor of rich exotic flowers,
& the women, Flor de Murias, dark
beauty with ringlets staring at her one
flower, pining for her lover,

the big-breasted Belinda
of the full-bodied double corona,
& her opposite, the pasty ingénue
who would date anyone, up for sale
on every Gloria Cubana, they could be
married for an hour or two, rescued
from a cellophaned life
by sliding money over a glass
countertop, beauties existing in wreathes
of smoke, sandalwood, burnt cherry,
notes of butternut & leather, on back
porches, & on summer evenings,
in the rings fathers blew for their children.

FERNS: A STUDY

From his pose in the garden
just as his voice became
my own Froebel stepped into the evening

of my dream for his uncommon love
of the young and with his notes
at the close of another century
collected from an elemental source
of children, my children of the forest
and the perpetual lily pond mad for the end,
playing and sometimes translucent
against the sun endowed with beauty
which has become commonplace
and for beauty's tension they never cease
from the pursuit of themselves
as though they inhabit this place
only to breed themselves to death by error.

As forests were once ferns
and ferns infant in the dumb morning
existing of notions
which were also geometries
copious among us

as they were always among us
even in the dreams of twelfth-century girls
dreaming at the edge of the forest
in anticipation of the unimagined season,

the caress and the still life
of ferns
on seacoasts and on the white porches
of summer homes
or hung from the platforms of wooden depots,
how they bowed along the boulevards
welcoming victors to the city,
and atop cool Corinthian planters
in the lobbies of grand hotels
there were ferns

in the background of photographs,
pharmacies and funeral parlors,
and in the corridors of museums
positioned carefully below milky skylights
that are sealed and permit no entry,

but most in a memory of children
there were ferns
copious, still and sometimes swaying
in the settings of their stories,
in the stories of their sleep.

EUNUCHS AT SUNRISE

Every morning they show up in the square,
singing in the sunrise.

They arrive in different patterns,
riding on each other's backs.

Somersaulting and leapfrogging,
they are from the eunuch orphanage

on the Hill of Stars outside of town,
that overlooks the ocean of air

there they are safe from everything
& every morning their number doubles.

The eternal eunuchs
singing in the sunrise.

In the ancient Egyptian pantheon,
the cult of Thoth, the god of scribes,
writing & other dominions, was not
extensive. Seshat was his female
counterpart.

THOTH

After all these years you would think
that you would have written to me,
to send some assurance that after
an honorable life,

I will not have to pay the ferryman
more than once, that I will be
judged worthy of some small grace,
a favorable review
where it counts, a reader or two
once I have passed, diviner of magic
& time, the moon, most underrated
of gods, I relate to you,
figure on my desk all gold & black
with head of the sacred ibis
(your bill competes with your stylus,)
be there at the weighing of my heart,
let it be no heavier than the feather
on the opposite scale
so that it won't be cast away
nor saved for some future life
such as I have known,
rather allow this soul
to live in fantasy, a dreaming
head in a dreaming dormitory
of wonder & felicity only
like some protozoan mindless of itself
among kindly forms all color & warmth,
say, eternal, glowing voyagers
complete with present sense,

without conscience or the grief
of this earth, let me be
without the need for words, or pen,
or reluctance, or bread & bone,
or this world, or friend.

SESHAT

I have seen you bathing
in the river under the moon,
Mistress of the Long House of Books.
Has your companion told you
about me?

Has he?
How I passed the test,
how my heart weighed well.
for this, surely, you, the loveliest
of your kind, could place a volume
of mine in a secure archive to be present
at the unveiling of the next universe,
or the next, complete, divine.

WINTER READING

The historic church packed, the poet,
famous, congenial, mythic & singular—
the atmosphere warmed by adulation
& after the last applause
faded into the dome,
& the spectacle
& spectators disappeared,
out on the cold pavement
in the parking lot
a crippled girl
who had put on lipstick
& rouge for the occasion,
in a wheel chair
surrounded by other students,
the teacher who brought her,
before she was lifted
into the van,
said, "Yes, I can do that.
Now I know what I want
to be," holding her manuscript
up to the moon.

WALT WHITMAN'S NOVEL

It is a Vivaldian summer passing
in verdant flashes, chlorophyll cells trembling
from rapid growth, then a child
comes to the door, she will uproot
weeds for a fee. At fourteen flat-chested
& podgy, her parent, working people,
promised her a horse on her twelfth birthday,
a companion. They have yet to make good,
& so she tells me of her new found calling,
she will draw the heads of horses,
travel from stable to stable,
she will do this for a fee.

How do we ever find our way? Must we each
have a labyrinth? An impossible design in green?
Walt's first book was a moral illustration
on intemperance & by the author's account
written in three days inspired by gin.
He did this for a fee.
From my window I see the child
who wants to travel town to town
in the garden pulling weeds.
I tell her she can stop,
pay her off, enough for a box of charcoals,
some paper, acid-free, well-made.

LOOKING FOR PICASSO ON EBAY

My wife loves art. It is her birthday.
Because of this, I am looking for Picasso
on eBay. Among the thousands
of lithographs signed & numbered
in pencil, I find 'Paloma sur fond rouge,'
& bid the balance of my bank account.

Now I am in electronic Picassoland,
among the mixed media, how prolific
he was, and varied, & how unlike
the literary artists, bound to one voice,
denied their periods during a life,
confined so often to a single *genre*.

But this does not matter to my wife.
She will frame this tortured thing
I have ordered, praising Picasso,
his artistic gluttony, his infant self,
how he left his true believers, the women,
a man after his own heart.

LA BELLE ÉPOQUE

After a fine arts degree from a college
with a name like a flower, my sister
worked for an art dealer until he went
out of business, and is now employed
by a local delicatessen owned by the same
person who owns the meat packing plant
where her son works, finishing a GED.

All the art in the world cannot feed a table,
she says, you are with the voice of your age,
or you can talk to yourself in a corner. Take it,
or leave it. This is no Belle Époque. It is political,
which means the beast is in costume. Read Vico.
But cultural values are recursive, aren't they?
I ask while she works on her son's hair,
shaping it into midnight-blue metallic spikes.

SEX EDUCATION

Like I tell my students, sex
invigorates. It is what we are
supposed to do with our lives,
but with caution. Use caution
like the colleague across the hall
who teaches punctuation, wondering
if a comma splice is more dangerous
than a colon. Then let go. And just
don't go out on the make, looking
for someone to bugger for buggering's
sake, make it mean something. Not like
that fuck of a swimming coach—who
should have been arrested years ago—
jumping into every pool, as if through
decades of countless affairs,
nameless faces that come & go,
you could keep yourself decent, complete,
not a mockery to self and soul.

PASSION BRACELET

A friend of mine was accused of infidelity
by his wife. He claimed it was her fault
for suggesting the passion bracelet in the first place,
the one that would re-energize their relationship.
After all, it was a balmy day and they were strolling
hand in hand through the mall when they found
the stand and inside the glass case was the bracelet
that would change their lives. It was incised
with symbols from Atlantis, made of zinc, copper
and tiny magnets to transform those ozone ions.
It was all too much, he explained, too much to control.
Passion does not know direction and that is why it is blind.
He asked for understanding, sympathy, time,
and while his wife was considering late that night,
the passion bracelet glowed when he went outside.

MY INTERNET FAMILY

It's not hard to do, not like picking up
after a baby brother all afternoon. Just
register. I did, then I was friended. In
a week, I had hundreds, pictures and
everything. I know it's just opinions
and gossip, but it's what everybody's
talking about. Even the news guy
on T.V. said social media is
so powerful kids kill themselves
over it. He called it the new gold
standard of our age, and who would
know better than him?

GOLD STARS

My niece won a certificate for gymnastics.
She is ten. Now she wants to be world class,
like the girls on television. I was the same way,
until my knee blew out, then I discovered
piercings, & now my goal is to have a studded face.
I get a discount because I work at an ink shop
& there's lots of trade going on. I could be
lizard lady. Who knows? Besides, even if you win
a gold medal in an event, unless you have
the personality to go with it, & become a broad-
caster or something, people forget. Like it goes down
a black hole. Don't tell this to the up-and-coming.
Most of the would-be's can't win for losing. Maybe
this isn't true for artists like my boss, but in sports,
it's different. Who's going to be vaulting when
they're fifty? Find something you can keep going with.
Besides, getting trashed isn't so bad. I tell my niece
I could get my boss to do her first tat for free.
Even stars trash themselves.

GEOGRAPHICS

On a switchback in the Catalinas we stopped
to catch our breath, leaned against our walking poles,
& to our right, upslope, a triangle of grasses
& shrubs with a dark streak from the melting snow
of two months ago, a *mons veneris*
that arcs & swells in spring, & this suggested
other formations: burial mounds that take the body
in whole, phallus of saguaro cactus,
clitoral pedernals, crooked thumb mountain,
the finger lakes, tulip head beach, crested butte,
crevasse & hoodoo, fertile crescents, colonic caves.
It is not always sex, but sex is what we see,
deltas where waters meet,
Psyche's shared symmetries.

BOOK OF SAND

In the home of a friend I find
a life-sized book with illustrations
of the world's beaches.

Sand-blonde beaches that sweep around
crossed rails of lost driftwood,
pockets of opal sand strung between

pools somewhere in secret Africa,
miles of salmon sand along
a coastline in New Zealand,

beaches of Russian black sand
& Mediterranean stretches
of purple-coral sand to take

in fingers & toes, backs & thighs,
running shadows, whole figures,
walking selves of sand.

ROLLER DERBY

Hurt's got the door tonight.
They put him on Security
or he'd just go after Rod-X
for hitting on Temp, his squeeze,
when she was benched
for a false start on a jam.

Besides, it's a packed house.
Cuff's the announcer, calls me
on the speakers all over the arena.
I play Calypso, his lost love slave.
Late in the second half we wave.
The crowd sighs.

A Wall of blockers slammed Angel
against the rails again. She sees
floating things. The team's
chipping in for an eye exam,
but it's probably in her head
from the hits & spills.

She does club prayer at half-time.
We make a circle, shoulder to shoulder,
huddle in tight, heads down low.
The fans love it, like the charity
we sponsor for kids with messed-up bones.
Community service is where it's at,

no one wants to believe we're only
bad girls, & know the put on,
like get past the tats, the black
fish net, the butt-flirting when we pack
up for the whistle, but the track
gets serious. Snap put an elbow

into Beaver Cleaver, a girl from the other
team, "Flower Bombers" for giving her
a crotch chop, backswinging the edge
of her hand as she passed,
a move the refs pretend not to notice,
& the crowd roars about the raw deal.

Lots of girls take it
for a couple of years, then drop out.
Some hang around, come to drills,
but when you're out, you're out.
Tribe's tribe. I mean, we're all
professionals. Trip's a tax lawyer,

tho' you'd never know it. Ms. Clitty
owns a physical therapy clinic, where we go
to get the knots out after practice. Ram-U, See?
is an anthropologist for the county
historical society. Mulch is a teach,
who tried last season to pass a Wall

& got flattened so bad, her collarbone broke,
but she's back at it. The fans love her more than ever.
There's always some kind of action going on.
Cuff announces the after party's at The Red Garter,
a local hot spot. Rod-X will take out
Hurt in the parking lot. Everyone's invited.

SLEEVES AT THE 13ᵗʰ STEP

I drop by after work. Not all the time,
not to be obvious, only when I know
Kari's on. If Guinness is $5.00,
I give her $7.00 & she thanks me
& smiles. That's enough.

No it's not. I want to know about
the sleeves. It took weeks to work up
the courage to ask. They're the places
she's been, NY, PA, NM,
& the shapes of the states are connected

by the vines of some oriental flower
because she wants to go to Japan.
There's a pod of pink dolphins
arched in ocean waves on her bicep.
"They're endangered," she explains, "like me."

There's the heart her father never had,
& of all of it, she says, "It's me.
It's who I am. Even if I get old
& get Alzheimer's some day
at least I'll know who I am."

MAGNIFICAT

The greatest statement ever made,
the *magnum opus* of all things,
is the manifest of desire.

Desire the perpetual, desire
the profound, the everywhere,
texts whistling
in the trees of Ceylon,
blowing up gulf coasts,

desire in the heart that ceases,
still as red coral, made so by it,
and in the heart that remains,
and in the dissolving pool
after the rain and in the rain.

It is the dumb giant gone
to the children's tea party,
the return of the lava avalanche
and the rarest mountain flowers,
the tsunami that washes out
generations, whole islands.

It is the earthly organism
cooperating with systems
here and beyond the moon,

while we stand, desire itself,
forever awash in bright danger.

STAIRCASE AT SCEAUX

—Mon projet aujourd'hui est d'être absorbé.

In the window of a shop in the *Passage des Panoramas,* (next year
it could be Prague, Budapest, or Riga,) the onlooker with the cape
over his arm, exposing a lining—it has been soiled—stares at
Kertész's photo of a staircase in Parc des Sceaux, all but a ruin
now, what memory left in exchange for silk ball gowns, early
evenings & gelatin-silver passages, & the partygoers, each with a
long-stemmed flower with glass petals, float about the scene in
black & white, mouths open in phatic chat, the moment eternal
in the open mouth, glass heart of history, they glide on invisible
rails up & down the steps meant to take strollers from lower to
higher ground & back again, (designed by André Le Nôtre,
responsible for the park at Versailles as well. Atget, a compulsive
photographer who wished to gather every image of Paris also
took photos of steps like these, but not from this angle of
abandonment, with such an abundance of curled leaves, & never as
haunting.) For now, there are the faces of passerbys on the
surfaces of bubbles passing over shop windows, rhizome of
reflections in the eyes of the onlooker, which are eyes of mirror,
faces floating over walls of polished granite, across the glass roof
of the arcade itself, the revolving images of strangers where he has
found a home among the homeless, having become them, the city,
the freedom of interchangeability, lost identity, album of the
arcade, a renewed body, Dreamer of days.

Parc des Sceaux, Paris, 1926, André Kertész

Michael Gessner, a former Andrew Mellon professor at the University of Arizona, and Honors Program director at Central Arizona College, lives in Tucson, Arizona with his wife, and their dog, "Irish." His work has been featured in *American Letters & Commentary*, *American Literary Review*, *The Journal of the American Medical Association*, *Oxford Magazine*, *The Wallace Stevens Journal*, *Web del Sol*, and others. His poems have been nominated twice for a Pushcart Prize and as finalists for "Discovery"/*The Nation*, and the Pablo Neruda Award. Other information, including book publications, reviews, and readings may be found at: www.michaelgessner.com, or www.pw.org/content/michael_gessner

Made in the USA
Middletown, DE
17 November 2020

24044640R00060